Power of a Woman Series

Living a Balanced Life

Dr. Cassundra White-Elliott

Living a Balanced Life is a work of non-fiction. However, in some of the testimonies, names have been changed to protect identities. All scriptures are from the King James Version of the Holy Bible.

CLF Publishing, LLC.
9161 Sierra Ave, Ste. 203C
Fontana, CA 92335
www.clfpublishing.org

Cover Design by Senir Design. Contact information- info@senirdesign.com.

ISBN# 978-1-945102-06-6

Printed in the United States of America.

Dedications

Dedicated with love to my cousins:
Bridget
&
Jade

Praising God for reuniting us!

Acknowledgements

In anticipation of an awesome 11th Annual Conference for International Women's Commission, where this book will be released, I humbly acknowledge my cabinet members: Millicent Redd, Deborah Reed-Hunter, Debbie Buckner, and Shelia Bryant-Colbert for all their assistance in creating an atmosphere for the women to be blessed!

TABLE OF CONTENTS

INTRODUCTION

Do you remember when your life seemed to be much simpler than it is today? How long ago were the simpler days exactly? Were they a few years ago? Were they when you were in college, high school, a teenager, or an adolescent? Do you remember being a teenager and earnestly wanting to be an adult, and everybody warned you not to grow up too quickly? Of course, this is not the case for all teenagers, but it probably is the case for the mass majority of them. Teens always seem to want to rush into adulthood, primarily to escape the authority of their parents. Teenagers, for some strange reason, think they can handle life on their own, with all of life's responsibilities.

One vital responsibility of adulthood is making sure you keep a handle on life (to the best of your ability), not allowing things to get out of hand emotionally, physically, financially, or psychologically. Adulthood carries many responsibilities, and as you increase your responsibilities, either with a career, with expenses, with children, or with a mate, you will also gain the potential to increase your stress level as well. With stress, life begins to lose its balance, as one circumstance may take your focus off others. If this situation is temporary, then you can return to living a balanced and productive life.

However, if the situation is prolonged or exacerbated, your life can begin to lose its balance and remain in that condition for an undetermined period of time. So, how does one correct this condition and/or prevent it from occurring in the first place? Living a balanced life simply begins with having the right perspective in all areas of your life, and those areas will vary from one person to the next. The components you have in your life may not be the same components your neighbors, coworkers, or family members have in their lives.

Throughout this book, I have pinpointed some areas that can potentially hinder anyone from having a balanced life. Before we delve into those specific areas, permit me to share with you how possessing the proper mindset is the foundation for setting everything else in place. If you do not have a healthy outlook on life with an equally healthy temperament, everything else will be in jeopardy. The Bible says as a man thinks so is he (Prov. 23:7). Whatever you spend time pondering and calculating will eventually play out in your life. Furthermore, that is why we are admonished to _not_ be conformed to this world but to be transformed by the renewing of our minds (Romans 12:2). Our minds must be renewed because of all the corrupt thinking in our present society.

To demonstrate what I mean by having a healthy perspective, let us turn our attention to the book of St. Luke Chapter 15. This specific chapter includes three parables (the topic of each parable is a lost item: the first is about the lost sheep, the second is about the lost coin, and the third is about the lost son, also known as the story of the prodigal son. Our focus is on the parable of the prodigal son (verses 11-32). Read the verses below.

Jesus continued: "There was a man who had two sons. [12] The younger one said to his father, 'Father, give me my share of the estate.' So he divided his property between them. [13] "Not long after that, the younger son got together all he had, set off for a distant country and there squandered his wealth in wild living. [14] After he had spent everything, there was a severe famine in that whole country, and he began to be in need. [15] So he went and hired himself out to a citizen of that country, who sent him to his fields to feed pigs. [16] He longed to fill his stomach with the pods that the pigs were eating, but no one gave him anything. [17] "When he came to his senses, he said, 'How many of my father's hired servants have food to spare, and here I am starving to death! [18] I will set out and go back to my father and say to him: Father, I have sinned against heaven and against you. [19] I am no longer worthy to be called your son; make me like one of your hired servants.' [20] So he got up and went to his father. "But while he was still a long way off, his father saw him and was filled with compassion for him; he ran to his son, threw his arms around him and kissed him. [21] "The son said to him, 'Father, I have sinned against heaven and against you. I am no longer worthy to be called your son.' *²²* "But the father said to his servants, 'Quick! Bring the best robe and put it on him. Put a ring on his finger and sandals on his feet. *²³* Bring the fattened calf and kill it. Let's have a feast and celebrate. *²⁴* For this son of mine was dead and is alive again; he was lost and is found.' So they began to celebrate. *²⁵* "Meanwhile, the older son was in the field. When he came near the house, he heard music and dancing. *²⁶* So he called one of the servants and asked him what was going on. *²⁷* 'Your brother has come,' he replied, 'and your father has killed the fattened calf because he has him back safe and sound.' *²⁸* "The older brother became angry and refused to go in. So his father went out and pleaded with him. *²⁹* But he answered his father, 'Look! All these years I've been slaving for you and never disobeyed your orders. Yet you never gave me even a young goat so I could celebrate with my friends. *³⁰* But when this son of yours who has squandered your property with prostitutes comes home, you kill the fattened calf for him!' *³¹* "'My son,' the father said, 'you are always with me, and everything I have is yours. *³²* But we had to celebrate and be glad, because this brother of yours was dead and is alive again; he was lost and is found.'"*

From this story, we can deduce three perspectives: the father's perspective, the older son/brother's perspective, and the perspective of the prodigal son (the younger/lost son).

Let's begin with the perspective of the prodigal son, as he is the antagonist in the story. The antagonist is the villain, the adversary, or simply put- the one who causes the problem or problems for others due to his egocentric or self-centered attitude. Now of course, the antagonist does not see himself this way. Instead, he believes he is levelheaded and on the right path, but in reality, his actions and thoughts cause harm to others.

In the case of the prodigal son, he requested his inheritance from his father. This request, in and of itself, demonstrates faulty thinking because how can one inherit anything when the holder of the goods is still alive? An inheritance is something you gain after one has passed from this life. Although the youngest son probably saw his request for his inheritance as no big deal, it truly demonstrated his self-centeredness, as he desired to obtain the inheritance for his own personal gain, for his own personal enjoyment, not for anyone else and not to give to a charity, but basically to line his own pockets. Also, the son carried the spirit of pride and a sense of entitlement. Both perspectives cause one to believe he or she is worthy or deserving of something although he or she has done nothing for which to be rewarded. The son gathered because he *was* the father's child, he was entitled to the father's wealth.

From the parable, the father did not appear to put up any resistance. He honored his youngest son's request, by dividing his property between his two sons. Shortly after, the younger son gathered his belongings and departed from home, with his destination being a foreign land. This action demonstrates his desire to be on his own, away from his father's rule, to do as he pleased. Upon his arrival, he began to have wild parties and indulge in wild living, spending his money frivolously. Before long, he found himself with no money or a means to support himself, while the foreign land experienced a famine. Consequently, he was required to find a way to feed himself. A farmer hired him to feed his livestock, namely the pigs. The son soon found himself dining with the pigs, as that was the only way he could sustain himself physically. So, the once wealthy young man became destitute.

While in his condition, he began to question his very surroundings and state of being. As he thought of his prior condition -living in the comfort of the family home- he remembered his father's servants and how they lived. There he was far away from home, working as a servant who had no substantial means to feed himself. While back at home, the servants were fed very well. Comparing the servants' living situation to his own, he thought it would be best to return to his father's house and see if he would be permitted to work as a servant. That way, he would have both shelter and food, in a warm and comfortable environment. He did not believe he deserved to carry the title 'son' any longer because of his previous behaviors, but he would welcome the position of servant. With his newfound mindset and a sense of humility, he set on his journey to return home.

Now, let us survey the father's perspective. The father was obviously a caring man because in addition to honoring his son's initial request for the inheritance, he cared for his son's well-being, thinking of him often and wondering if he was safe and well. Although the son left and failed to keep in fellowship and communication with his family, the father wished no harm upon him. He looked for his son to return home, day in and day out, but the son failed to do so- until the predetermined day. On that day, the father looked down the road and from afar off, he saw his son approaching the family home. The father was filled with joy and immediately told the servants to prepare a feast, and to bring a robe and ring to adorn the younger son.

The father's behavior and attitude were those that were normally projected towards a person of high honor, status and respect, not of someone who walked away without even a glance back or a letter or phone call to inform him of his well-being. The father demonstrated unconditional love, even when that same love, care, and concern was not demonstrated towards him. He did not walk in unforgiveness or bitterness. He kept his heart and mind pure towards his son because he truly only wanted the best for him.

Now, let us survey the brother's perspective. The older son/brother was obviously dedicated to his father because he was present when the younger son left, and he was still present when the younger son returned. However, he did not share the same feelings his father did. He was appalled at all that had occurred and his father's actions. He did not understand why he never received the same treatment that his brother was presently experiencing when his brother had run off with his inheritance and squandered it, but he had been the responsible one, remaining by his father's side and doing as he was asked. His father explained he did not need to be rewarded for doing what was right, but his brother who had left without a word afterword had been presumed dead to never return. So, upon his return, he was to be celebrated and welcomed back.

The older son felt the father's treatment of the two sons was unfair and insensible. His comments demonstrated the envy he beheld towards his brother and the discontent he held for his father. His feelings were so deeply engrained that he refused to go into the feast and celebrate with the others.

The mindset of the two sons can contribute to an imbalanced life. The mindset of the younger son caused him to leave a secure environment for one that was volatile and unstable. What would he have done to get his life back on course if his father had not welcomed him back with open arms? We cannot live life on a day-to-day basis without a viable plan. From our own experiences as well as those of others, we know that even a good plan can go wrong, so why would we operate with no plan at all? That is what the prodigal son did. He took what he had and lived a wild, carefree life for as long as he could with no plan for after the funds ran out. He had no one he could count on in the world, except his father. With his father's love, care, and concern, he was able to have a second chance. But, the reality is- second chances do not always come.

The mindset of the older son can only lead to destruction. The parable did not tell what happened to the family after the night of the feast, but we can only imagine. The prodigal son hoped he would be at least able to serve his father in the role of a servant, but we know the father received him back into the role he was born into- son. Therefore, their relationship was instantly restored. However, if the older son's disposition remained, he could have carried the root of bitterness on for an undetermined period of time. If this were the case, other unclean spirits would undoubtedly branch from the root and develop in his life. The root of bitterness, unforgiveness, envy, jealousy, spite, and pride could take over his life and ruin his relationship with both his father and brother. These negative emotions could lead to unhealthy behavioral traits and cause disruption in his life that could be difficult to break away from down the line.

The father's mindset was the healthiest mindset of the three. Because he had a heart to forgive and to love, he not only kept his own life balanced with healthy emotions, but he was able to be of further assistance to his younger son. The father is an example to each of us because we all have had someone treat us in an unfair manner to one degree or another. But the question is, "How did we respond?" Our response is what either keeps our life balanced or causes imbalance. We have the power to walk in love, forgiveness, kindness, gentleness, longsuffering, and joy. How we respond to a situation or to a person will have an impact on what happens next. Also, how we plan or fail to plan will also have an impact on the balance or lack thereof that we experience in our lives.

The following chapters will discuss and uncover a variety of topics that many people have allowed to cause imbalance in their lives. Sometimes, imbalance is unpreventable. But, prolonged imbalance must be dealt with because it is unhealthy in and of itself and can lead to other unhealthy patterns in our lives. Once you discover any patterns of imbalance in your life, it is your duty to correct it, so that your life is unencumbered and your mind is clear. This will enable you to hear from God and prevent you from missing anything He has for you!

CHAPTER ONE

Letting Go of the Past

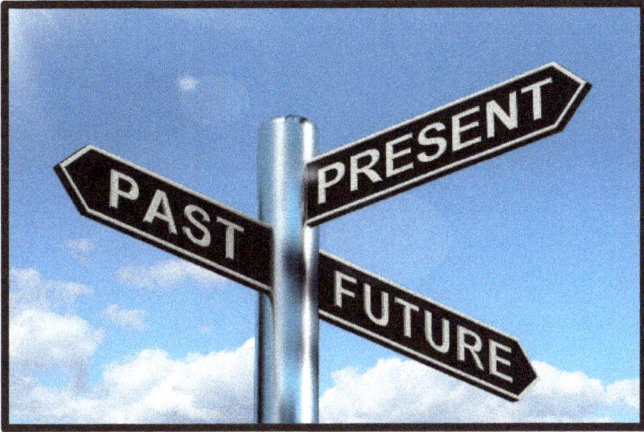

Everyone has a past, a present, and a future. It is impossible to live in all three time frames at the same time. The past is to be learned from and the memories are to be treasured. The present is to be enjoyed and used to make more memories and as learning moments for the future. The future is to be planned for, so it is not squandered.

The problem that can arise with the past is people tend to get stuck in it, and as a result, the present seems to slip by, and the future is bound to be wasted as well.

Our past consists of great and wonderful times as well as hurtful disappointing times, but they are all for our learning. If mistakes or missteps were made, we learn how the missteps occurred and figure out how not to make the same ones again. If successes were gained, we celebrate those and see if and how they can be replicated.

When we take a look into the past, we can see that it isn't the wonderful, joyous occasions that debilitate us. Rather, it is the seasons of hurt that may debilitate us from moving forward along the path that God predestined for us. Hurtful times tend to be the most debilitating because people tend to dwell more on their mistakes, failures, and disappointments than any other type of incident. They tend to beat themselves up rather than using the incident(s) as learning opportunities for future growth and development. Consequently, as they ponder and reflect on the past *continuously*, they miss out on the present and fail to plan for the future.

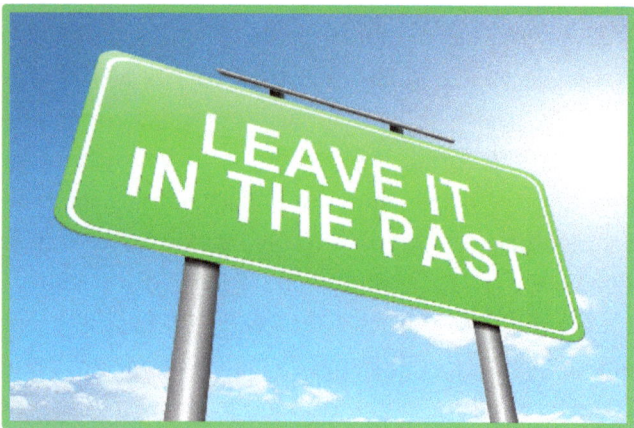

In an interview with Debbie Buckner, she revealed some important points that work for her as it relates to letting go of the past. According to Debbie, when dealing with relationships, our past can hinder us when we allow our hurts and past relationships to dictate our behavior, our feelings, and our thoughts, while in a new relationship. For example, if we were in a wonderful relationship, and our mate had the utmost respect for us and treated us very lovingly and kindly, but for one reason or another, the relationship ended, we may be impacted if we are not watchful. As time passes, we may find ourselves in another relationship. Once we enter that relationship, we cannot expect the person with whom we are in this new relationship with to do the exact same things and have the exact same mannerisms and temperament as our past partner.

Conversely, if we experience a negative relationship with a person, we cannot hold what happened in that relationship against the next person we have a relationship with or even be unfair to that person by holding back our feelings because we may fear being hurt. We must allow the past to stay in the past, whether it was good or bad.

Apostle Paul says, in Philippians 3:13-14: *"Brethren, I count not myself to have apprehended: but this one thing I do, forgetting those things which are behind, and reaching forth unto those things which are before, I press toward the mark for the prize of the high calling of God in Christ Jesus."* Apostle Paul warns us about focusing on the past. He says we should leave those things behind and reach toward what is in front of us. If we find ourselves focused on what 'used to be' instead of dealing with 'what is,' we will miss out on what God has for us.

Furthermore, Debbie shared a financial dilemma she faced some time ago and the impact it had on her life. After graduating high school, Debbie was able to obtain a job that paid $65,000 a year. She was very pleased with that taking place in her life, not only because the amount of money allowed her to pay her bills and do the things she desired, but also because she was able to obtain the job without a college degree. However, time passed, and Debbie found herself without that job. Losing her job placed her into a position of having to file for General Relief, a government program that helps those who are without employment. Later, Debbie also found herself homeless, moving from residence to residence, with friends and family. Now, Debbie is doing much better, by the grace of God, and she has learned that all disappointing situations do not last always. Why not? Because, God always has a ram in the bush!

As I closed the interview with Debbie, she also mentioned a specific incident with dealing with the past that really touched me. She shared with me how devastated she was when her only son was incarcerated. She said although it has been 17 years, she remembers it as though it were yesterday. The incident took place on a Mother's Day, and for years, Debbie refused to celebrate Mother's Day. Some of you may be able to sympathize with Debbie and her feelings of despair. However, before you sympathize too quickly, let me share this: Debbie was not only the mother of her son, but she also has two daughters who love her as much as her son does. How do you think the daughters felt when their mother did not want to celebrate? She is the only mother they have and, as other children, they wanted to be able to make their affections known. I'm not saying Debbie prevented them from doing so, but just think about the impact her attitude/behavior had on them. Now, where do you stand?

We must always be cognizant of the world around us. We do not live in bubbles, and it is not fair to shut others out. Thankfully, Debbie has moved past the past and does not harbor the same feelings as she once did. She has broken free from the bondages of the past and looks at her present and to her future with a renewed mindset. As the Word says in Romans 12:2: *"And be not conformed to this world: but be ye transformed by the renewing of your mind, that ye may prove what is that good, and acceptable, and perfect, will of God."*

In many situations, we will find ourselves conforming to the mindsets and attitudes of the secular society in which we reside. These mindsets and attitudes can be to our detriment. Therefore, we must be careful to adhere to the Word of God, not only in this situation, but in all situations. Debbie's mind had to go through a transformation. She had to see through the eyes of faith and know that God has so much more in store for her. She is not limited by her past. What a breakthrough that realization enabled her to have!

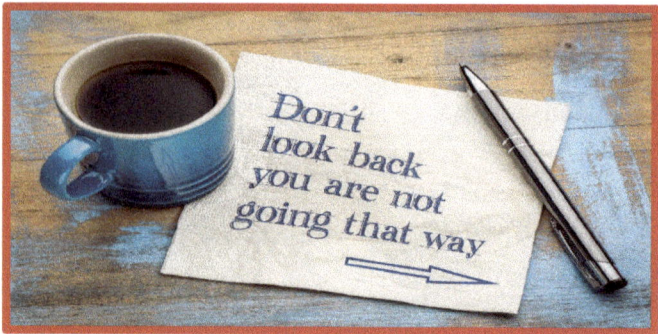

The following excerpt on letting go of the past can be found in my book *Dare to Succeed:*

God's holy Word tells us in Isaiah 43: 18-19, *"Remember ye not the former things, neither consider the things of old. Behold, I will do a new thing; now it shall spring forth; shall ye not know it? I will even make a way in the wilderness, and rivers in the desert."* This scripture tells us plainly that we are not to focus on what happened to us in the past. God promises that He will do a new thing. Then, He asks us whether or not we know that He will. He is asking us whether or not we have faith in Him and believe that He will change our situation or make our future bright regardless of our past hurts. Then, He goes on to say that He *will* make a way in the wilderness. So, even though we may be overwrought with confusion and do not know where to turn, He directs us by telling us to turn to Him and let Him take care of the past, the present, and the future.

CHAPTER TWO

Eradicating Low Self-Esteem

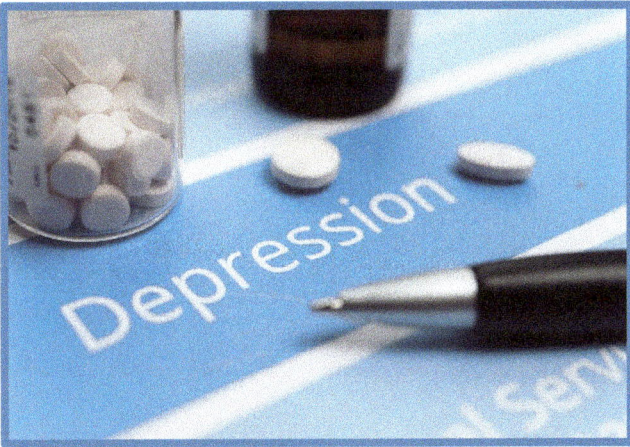

Depression is another commonly experienced negative emotion and is often caused by the spirit of low self-esteem. When we harbor unforgiveness in our hearts, we may begin to internalize the words that have been spoken in someone's effort to tear down our self-worth. However, it is not what man says about us that should concern us. We should be concerned about who God says we are. In Romans 12:3, Paul warns that we should not think more highly of ourselves than what we actually are. He says, *"For I say, through the grace given unto me, to every man that is among you, not to think of*

himself more highly than he ought to think; but to think soberly, according as God hath dealt to every man the measure of faith." Also inherent in this verse is the converse notion that we should not think lower of ourselves. We should know exactly who we are.

God highly esteemed us before we departed from our mother's womb. He thought of us before we were ever created. The Bible tells us that man was created on the six day, after everything else was created and before God rested. Genesis 2:2-3 tells us how God rested on the seventh day after He created the universe, and Genesis 2:7 tells us that man was formed from the dust from the ground. However, if we back track to Chapter One of Genesis, we find that God already had the idea of creating man because the Word says, *"And God said, Let us make man in our image, after our likeness: and let them have dominion over the fish of the sea, and over the fowl of the air, and over the cattle, and over all the earth, and over every creeping thing that creepeth upon the earth. So God created man in his own image, in the image of God created he him; male and female created he them"* (Genesis 1:26-27).

From these verses, we can see that low self-esteem is not the result of God placing us low on the totem pole of the earthly hierarchy; instead, it is the result of negative patterns. The following behaviors are characteristic of low self-esteem. As you read through them, see if you possess any of them.

1. **Indulging in self-criticism.**
    The enemy does an excellent job of criticizing you. Do not join his team and help in the criticism.

2. **Neglecting personal needs by constantly seeking to please others.**
    It is great to be considerate of others, but do not neglect yourself.

3. **Trying to emulate someone else's style.**
    God created each one of us to be a unique individual. Be proud of who you are.

4. **Taking failures and the presence of problems too seriously**.
    Failure means you have not succeeded *yet*. Keep trying or alter the plan, but do not give up.

5. **Living life by conditions and terms set by other people.**
    God is the one who set the standard for our lives. Living life as you choose with God's guidelines, without hurting others, is not a sin. What may be good for someone else may not be good for you.

6. **Failing to recognize successes.**

   Focus on your accomplishments to demonstrate to yourself that you are capable of succeeding.

7. **Speaking negatively.**

   Proverbs 18:21a says, *"Death and life are in the power of the tongue."* Speak life into your own situation by saying positive affirmations. Do not speak negative words because they breed death.

8. **Focusing on past failures.**

   Learn from past mistakes, but let the past stay in the past.

To eliminate negative patterns that breed low self-esteem, which leads to deeper depression, unhappiness, insecurity, and poor confidence, read the following scriptures to see what God says about us in Psalms 8:3-9. *"When I consider thy heavens, the work of thy fingers, the moon and the stars, which thou hast ordained; What is man, that thou art mindful of him? and the son of man,*

that thou visitest him? For thou hast made him a little lower than the angels, and hast crowned him with glory and honour. Thou madest him to have dominion over the works of thy hands; thou hast put all things under his feet: All sheep and oxen, yea, and the beasts of the field; The fowl of the air, and the fish of the sea, and whatsoever passeth through the paths of the seas. O Lord our Lord, how excellent is thy name in all the earth!"

God thinks highly of us. His positioning of us over all His creation tells us that. We are positioned just lower than the angels, those who God keeps in His divine company. Rejoice in knowing how special and valuable we are to the creator of the universe.

Now, with the weapon of God's Word as our defense mechanism, we can use the following five steps to counteract low self-esteem and replace it with a healthy self-esteem.

1. **Face your fears.**

   They are not as bad as you think they are. Facing your fears increases your confidence.

2. **Forget your failures.**

   Learn from your failures. Avoid making the same mistakes again, but do not limit yourself by assuming you failed before so you cannot succeed the next time. Try again; you are wiser and stronger. Do not get trapped in the past!

3. **Know what you want and ask for it.**

   You deserve your dreams to come true.

4. **Reward yourself when you succeed.**
   No one else will.
5. **Don't be defeated.**
   Try something else.

(Perera, 2003)

Self-esteem is related to our self-worth and our value. Building esteem is a first step towards having joy and a better life. Self-esteem increases our confidence. If we have confidence, we will respect ourselves. If we respect ourselves, we can respect others; improve our relationships; our achievements; and our happiness (Perera, 2003).

David said in Psalms 139:14-16, *"I will praise thee; for I am fearfully and wonderfully made: marvellous are thy works; and that my soul knoweth right well. My substance was not hid from thee, when I was made in secret, and curiously wrought in the lowest parts of the earth. Thine eyes did see my substance, yet being unperfect; and in thy book all my members were written, which in continuance were fashioned, when as yet there was none of them."*

Remember David's words as he speaks of how God made us. Our individuality is to be celebrated, not denied, not rejected, and not cast away. Even if the words that are spoken to us are in reference to past acts that we may have committed that were contrary to God's Word, we should ask God for forgiveness and move on, leaving the past in the past. Bringing up the past is a trick of the enemy. Don't let it be a weapon against you. Continue to fight the good fight of faith, accept God's forgiveness, and celebrate yourself as a new creature.

Read this prayer aloud and rejoice in your uniqueness.

Father God,

I thank you Lord for creating me in your image, yet as one of a kind. I thank you for making me unique. I will walk tall and proud because I am a child of the Most High God. I am a child of you God, the creator of the universe. I will love me as you made me and as you re-create me, for somewhere along the way I have strayed from being just who you want me to be. Help me to not conform to the cares of this world, but to be transformed by the renewing of my mind. Renewing my mind comes from knowing what your Word says about me.

Help me to deprogram what the world says I should be and to look only to you so that you can guide me to become who you have called me to be. Oh Lord, direct my paths and keep me on the path of the righteous so that I may glorify you and give you much joy. Father God, please continue to watch over me, keeping me covered with your precious blood that protects me from the negative words spoken by those around me. Keep the negative words from penetrating my heart so that my heart will remain pure and not turn stony. Father, I thank you and I love you.

In Jesus' mighty name,

Amen.

(Excerpt taken from *Dare to Succeed* by
Dr. C. White-Elliott)

CHAPTER THREE

The Challenges of Blended Families

When two people decide to get married, and one or both of them have children, the two families become one blended family. It is enough for the two adults to go through the process of learning each other's likes, dislikes, mannerisms, behavior patterns, personalities, etc. But, to add in learning the same about the children that come with the mate is an added requirement.

Engaging with stepchildren can possibly, but not always, present certain dilemmas. There can be issues with the child's other biological parent, issues of jealousy/insecurity on the part of the child may arise due to you being a new component in the parent's life, there can be resistance to proffered discipline, behavior/ attitude problems may arise, etc.

Then, the way you opt to handle any of these instances may differ from that of the biological/natural parent. That, in and of itself, can cause problems in the new relationship, resulting in an imbalance in what could otherwise be a very happy, loving relationship.

A person's child is very dear to his/her heart, as the child is his/her flesh, blood, and bones. If the child is uncomfortable or unhappy, that creates discomfort and discontent within the biological parent. Then, the parent is forced to act in order to decide the best course of action to rectify or at least mollify the situation. To gain greater insight to the novelty of blended families, I conducted two interviews to gain information on the best way to deal with some of the discomfort that may arise within a blended family.

When looking to address the topic of blended families, I found the perfect candidate to interview: Cherice. I found her to be the perfect candidate because she has a twofold experience with blended families. She began her interview by sharing with me the interesting fact that she grew up in a blended family. Her mother had five children before giving birth to Cherice, and her father had five children of his own before he and Cherice's mother created her. The children each parent had were not with each other but were with other mates; therefore, Cherice is the only child whom her two parents have in common. And, she is the youngest of all her ten siblings.

Growing up, the experience that Cherice had when it came to interacting with her siblings was not what a normal child would desire. All of her siblings were much older (at least 17 years) than she; therefore, she grew up as an only child in her household. To compound matters, her parents divorced and married other people. Then, she went from being the only child to having stepparents whom she could either develop a relationship with or not. Cherice opted to retain close relationships with her natural parents and casual relationships with her stepparents, ensuring them they would not serve as replacements for the two who gave birth to her.

When I asked Cherice about her relationship with her siblings, she stated she basically has a better relationship with her mother's children than her father's. But, because all of them were so much older than she,

she didn't really have an opportunity to forge a 'normal' relationship with any of them.

Then, as fate would have it, Cherice married Jeffrey, who is the father of six children. Cherice herself has three teenage daughters from a previous relationship. She and her husband Jeffrey have no children in common, but they have a total of nine children.

Presently, in their household resides Jeffrey, Cherice, her three daughters, and Jeffrey's youngest daughter (a twenty year old). Now being the adult in the situation of a blended family, fulfilling the role of the mother to all four girls, Cherice tries very hard to keep the peace between her husband and her daughters. Not to imply that the situation is volatile, but you know how teenagers can be- especially, when they are accustomed to having just one parent and then, all of a sudden, they have two in the home.

Oftentimes, Cherice finds herself being the referee. Not only does she have to referee when she is present at home, but also when she is away from home. For example, when she is at work, it is not uncommon for her to receive a phone call regarding something that is not going smoothly in the home. The situation has become so exacerbated that she has even considered moving her girls out of the home and living separately from her husband, whom she loves dearly.

Although all four girls who reside in the house get along well, sometimes Cherice's three girls demonstrate feelings of insecurity and/or disapproval with the closeness Cherice shares with her husband's youngest daughter. Cherice ensures them, through her words and actions, that no one can take her away from them. She also tries to get them to understand that Jeffrey's daughter needs Cherice in the same ways they need her- even though she has a mother of her own. While Cherice's relationship with her stepdaughter is strong and healthy, her daughters' relationship with their stepfather Jeffrey is not as secure. This has proven to be problematic time and time again. What the end result will be- only time will tell.

Trying to find a healthy balance in the blended family can be quite the challenge from Cherice's first-hand experience. Her answer to keeping peace in the home and keeping her sanity is steadily seeking the Lord and staying constantly in prayer.

On the same topic of blended families, I interviewed Aretha Edwards regarding her marriage to Derrick Edwards and the blended family that came as a result. Derek is the father of eight children, and Aretha is the mother of four children, and they have no children in common. When Aretha and Derek joined together in holy matrimony, Aretha's four children were older teenagers and young adults and did not live in the home with her and her new husband. Conversely, Derek had several young children, and many of them would often visit and spend nights in their home. For Aretha, dealing with young children meant dealing with their mothers. This proved to be a challenging situation for Aretha, placing her in circumstances that she had never been involved in before.

Many of the women, who had children by her husband prior to her marrying him, still desired a relationship with him. This made their interaction tricky. There were four different mothers, and one of the mothers, who has three of the eight children, elected to keep the children away from their father simply because he had a new wife. On the other hand, there was another mother who also had three children, and those three children interacted with Aretha and Derrick, their father, on a regular basis.

Aretha chose to handle her involvement with the mothers and her interaction with the children in a godly manner. Did this happen overnight? Of course not. It was a process, and it took the leading of the Holy Spirit. There are several steps Aretha took to keep peace among everyone and for her own sanity.

First, she held the mindset that everyone has a past, and she could not hold her husband's past against him, even though it was currently impacting her present. The four women and the eight children pre-dated their relationship, and she understood that and dealt with it accordingly.

Second, she understood that she and her husband, as a result of holy matrimony, were one in Christ and whatever impacted him also impacted her. Did she enjoy everything that impacted her? Unfortunately, she did not, but she kept her head uplifted and had an ear to hear what the Spirit of the Lord had to say. On one occasion, the Holy Spirit revealed to her the course of her own actions and set her on the right course. Note- it is always important to see what role we play, if any, in the circumstances we are involved in.

Third, she accepted her husband's children into her life. As a result, the three daughters who would come on a regular basis developed a strong relationship with her.

Fourth, overtime, Aretha developed a relationship with the three daughters' mother by inviting her to church. In the midst of the daughters' mother going to church, some problems arose because this particular woman still had a desire for Derek although he was, at that point, a married man. Through it all, Aretha rested in the security of knowing that Derrick was dedicated to her, and she allowed that truth along with the faith she had in God to direct her paths and order her steps. Psalm 37:23 says, *"The steps of a good man are ordered by the LORD: and he delighteth in his way."*

Fifth, to keep order in their home, despite chaos caused by the children's mothers, Aretha and Derek spoke with the children and explained to them that they needed to respect the rules and guidelines that had been set forth in their home. Doing so brought an understanding between all of them and respect followed. This help to cut down on episodes of defiance and confusion.

The journey that Aretha had to take through the course of navigating through a blended family was not easy, but she proved it was doable. With God by her side and with God leading her, she could not fail. Another key to her success was taking her marriage vows seriously. The Bible says a three-stranded cord is not easily broken. (Ecclesiastes 4:12: *"A person standing alone can be attacked and defeated, but two can stand back-to-back and conquer. Three are even better, for a triple-braided cord is not easily broken."*) Aretha saw her husband and herself as one flesh, and even though she had trials and tribulations that she had to suffer through, she was determined to be steadfast and unmovable, as it related to her relationship.

Getting married is an exciting time for couples, and the beginning is a time where they are focused on building their life together. However, if the two parties have children from prior relationships, they must take into account the children's feelings and emotions when they decide to join their families together.

Many couples attend premarital counseling sessions before walking down the aisle, and it would be a good idea to include their children in some of those sessions. In doing so, they can head off any potential problems prior to saying 'I do.' Even after the vows have been made, when problems appear on the horizon, parents must be wise to address the problems as soon as they are noticed under the surface. Do not wait until the problems are in full force. They should deal with them as soon as they begin to bubble up under the surface.

Parents, for the sake of your children, know who you are marrying and know how he/she feels about your children- before you decide to marry him/her. This particularly pertains to children who will be in the home because they will be under the authority of your new spouse.

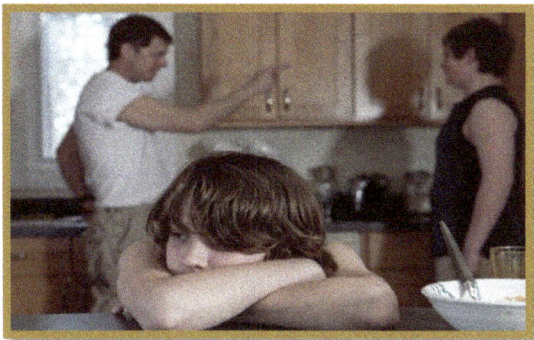

Here are several keys shared by the Empowering Parents Organization that will assist in effectively interacting and co-parenting stepchildren when you have a blended family:

1. **Defer to the Bio-Parent**

   Maintaining your presence and at the same time supporting the bio-parent may be difficult, but it will be productive. Remember, the bio-parent knows the child much better than you do and should know the best way to handle situations that involve his/her child. Therefore, he/she should make the major decisions that will impact the child. The irony is that when you relax and support the bio-parent, the relationship with your stepchild will form faster.

2. **Don't Compete with Your Counterpart**

   Uphold and respect them. In other words, don't try to be a better mom than your stepkids' bio-mom or a better dad than their bio-dad. No matter what you think of the bio-parent's style of discipline (or lack thereof), it's important to respect and acknowledge the strength of the biological connection.

3. **Discover Your Stepchild's Interests**

   Discover the things your stepson or stepdaughter likes. Start off as you would with any friendship: find some common ground and do things together that you might both enjoy. Remember, you're just there to build a relationship appropriately, not to parent or take the place of your stepchild's mother or father. Come in as a friend or a benevolent aunt or uncle; in other words, choose a role other than "parent" in order to foster the relationship.

4. **Get Out of the Way**

   Let your spouse have one-on-one time with his or her kids—*without you*. This helps reduce the displacement and loss the child might be feeling, and assures him/her that he/she hasn't been displaced by somebody else.

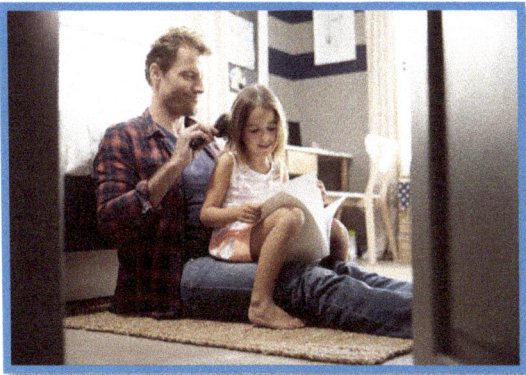

5. **Act Lovingly- Even If You Don't Like Your Stepkids**

It has been said quite often: "I feel guilty because I don't love my stepkids." The reality is that you may never love them as your own—or even like them. And remember, you can't make your stepkids like you, either! You are the "intruder." In their minds, you've displaced them. But even if you don't like them, you can learn to act lovingly toward them. Love is an action, so behave in a loving manner toward your stepkids. It may surprise you down the road. As the relationship develops, love just may develop!

CHAPTER FOUR

Education

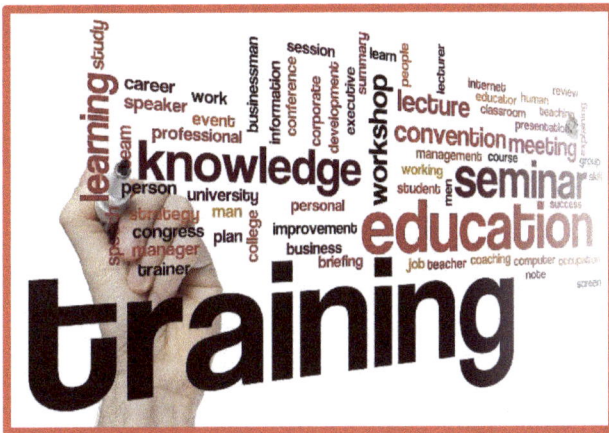

Education, whether obtained formally or informally, is the key to one's personal advancement. Therefore, when one fails to gain education, in any form, he/she will fail to grow or advance, causing imbalance in his/her life. For example, if a person's job or career, family, church commitments, and extracurricular activity consume all of his/her time, leaving no time for education, his/her life will be imbalanced.

On the other hand, when a person only focuses on gaining more and more knowledge, while failing to focus on life's other responsibilities, imbalance can also occur.

For example, if a person's educational pursuits are his/her only focus, leaving all of the responsibilities to falter, his/her life will also experience imbalance.

In a recent interview that I conducted with Felicia Watts, I asked her to share with me her overall thoughts about education. She shared her personal opinion, which emanates from her experiences: Education helps individuals have an open mind, develop opinions, and have varied points of view. Education also reemphasizes information we may have already attained when we revisit previously studied topics. Furthermore, education fosters critical thinking; whereby, we can process information more quickly and effectively, as well as make wiser decisions. Felicia considers herself a lifelong learner who enjoys taking in new pieces of information that will aid in brightening her horizons and making her more knowledgeable about the Word of God, so she will not be taken off course by worldly systems. Her foundational scripture for that train of thought comes from II Corinthians 4:6, which says, *"For God, who commanded the light to shine out of darkness, hath shined in our hearts, to give the light of the knowledge of the glory of God in the face of Jesus Christ."*

Moreover, I asked Felicia her perspective on having *a balanced life* as it pertains to education, looking at it from both sides of the spectrum. One side of the spectrum consists of those who seek education excessively to the detriment of their other responsibilities. The other side consists of those who allow other responsibilities to prevent them from gaining formal education. Felicia responded: Neither situation is healthy. It is important for every individual to have a balance in life as it pertains to education. Education is critical to our existence as humans. We cannot give up everything for education, by neglecting other responsibilities. At the same time, we cannot allow life's circumstances and other responsibilities to prevent us from gaining education. Therefore, each individual must find a way to gain knowledge on a regular basis without neglecting everything else God has placed into our hands. Doing so will allow our lives to be balanced with our information, thus enabling us to be well-rounded individuals.

The following excerpt on education can be found in my book *Through the Storm:*

Personally, I believe that whatever a person's educational desire is, he/she should strive to attain it. We know that the Bible says, *"My people are destroyed for lack of knowledge*" (Hosea 4:6a). I am a firm believer that the Bible is not only referring to knowledge of biblical principles. I believe that although we are not of this world, we must live in it, and in order to function to our fullest capacity, we must be knowledgeable about earthly things. Therefore, in an effort to not perish from a lack of knowledge, we must equip ourselves with mental ammunition.

Although attending school and earning degrees is not for everyone, knowledge should be everyone's friend, and we should put our knowledge to work for us. Throughout the 31 chapters of Proverbs, Solomon constantly reminds us to not be a fool because, "*A fool's talk brings a rod to his back, but the lips of the wise protect them*" (Proverbs 14:3). Solomon also tells us to, "*Stay away from a foolish man, for you will not find knowledge on his lips*" (Proverbs 14:7).

According to dictionary.net, a fool is, "One destitute of reason, or of the common powers of understanding; an idiot; a natural; 2. a person deficient in intellect; one who acts absurdly, or pursues a course contrary to the dictates of wisdom; one without judgment; a simpleton; a dolt; 3. one who acts contrary to moral and religious wisdom; a wicked person." Many agree with the first definition which states that a fool is someone who lacks common sense.

I prefer the third definition. From this definition and from Solomon's examples of the fool's behavior, a fool is not someone who lacks sound judgment or information. No, a fool is someone who is mentally capable of making sound decisions and, in most cases, has the information to do so, but chooses not to. A person who does not have sufficient information to make informed decisions on a topic is simply ignorant about the topic. One is considered to be ignorant when he/she lacks information. A fool, on the other hand, has the information and does not apply it.

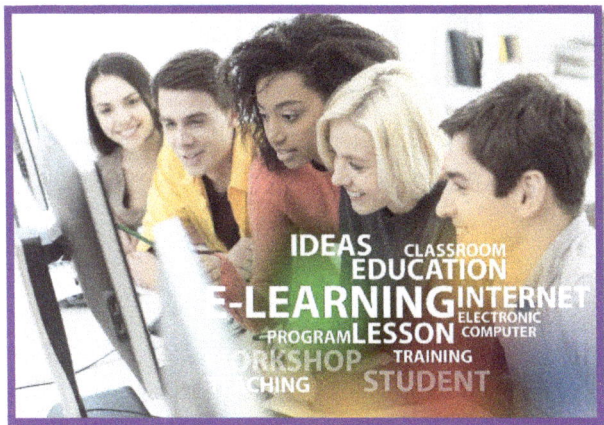

So, it is time to hold up the stop sign for the enemy. Stop allowing him to lie to you about your being too old to go back to school. Stop letting him tell you that you cannot afford it. Stop allowing him to tell you that you are not smart enough. Education is not about being smart; it is about having endurance to finish the race. Trust me, *once* I questioned my ability to finish my doctorate, but I stopped myself and said, "Oh no! The devil is not going to lead me down the path of doubting myself. I am equipped and capable to finish the task." Some of you need to boldly declare the same thing.

Let's do a faith-building exercise. Repeat the following words that are taken from an excerpt by Marianne Williamson:

Our deepest fear is not that we are inadequate. Our deepest fear is that we are powerful beyond measure. It is our light, not our darkness that most frightens us. We ask ourselves, "Who am I to be brilliant, gorgeous, talented, fabulous?" Actually, who are you *not* to be? You are a child of God. Playing small does not serve the world. There is nothing enlightened about shrinking so that other people won't feel insecure around you. We are all meant to shine, as children do. We were born to make manifest the glory of God that is within us. It's not just in some of us; it's in everyone. And as we let our own light shine, we unconsciously give other people permission to do the same. As we are liberated from our own fear, our presence automatically liberates others.

Now read it again, but this time, make it personal by referring to yourself. "My deepest fear is not that I am inadequate. My deepest fear….." Whenever you feel the spirit of fear creeping in to tell you what you cannot do, recite the words of Williamson's excerpt.

Educational success can be yours!

Just reach up and take hold!

CHAPTER FIVE

Dealing with Naysayers

All our lives we tend to have three categories of people in which we engage. First, there is a group of supporters they are always by our side, encouraging us to take on the desires of our hearts. Second, there are the silent bystanders, who don't say anything one way m or the other. They do not encourage us, nor do they discourage us from pursuing anything we may desire to pursue.

Finally, the third group is the naysayers. A naysayer is one who speaks words of discouragement aiming to turn you away from the task at hand. If you take heed to what the naysayers are saying in your life you will certainly encounter imbalance from settling and not pursuing your most heartfelt desires. There are several ways you can change the naysayer's discouraging words to benefit you.

1. **Repeat the naysayer's comment and follow-up with a question:**

   If you tell someone your idea for a new eatery downtown, and the person says, "Are you crazy? Restaurants always fail within the first year!" You can say, "Restaurants always fail with in the first year? Tell me then, what advice do you have to make sure mine doesn't fail?" This makes his defenses fall and will also bring out any experience he may have- or perhaps he will give you an idea of where to go for advice. If he cannot justify his 'nay,' then perhaps it's just pure naysaying.

2. **Let a naysayer know you want to hear his/her idea:**

   Naysayers are used to being dismissed. If you allow them to share their ideas, it makes them less defensive. This may also give you a new idea or another perspective.

3. **Compliment the naysayer's suggestions:**
   You could turn a naysayer into an ally by letting her know she is appreciated. It is rare for a negative person to be complimented, so you can throw her off by making a positive reply. She is not expecting your gracious words- a little bit of reverse psychology, huh? You don't have to take her up on her ideas; you will just simply compliment her. She may think twice about being negative with you again because it did not work out the first time!

4. **If it doesn't apply, let it fly:**
   Sometimes, even after letting a naysayer be heard, it may not be something positive. If it doesn't apply, let it fly! Meaning, forget it was said and move on.

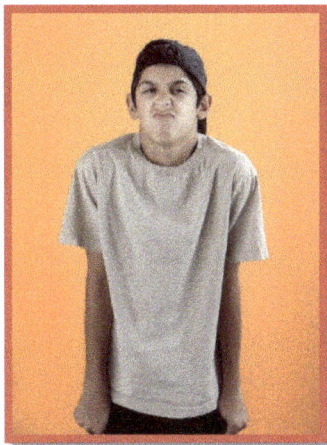

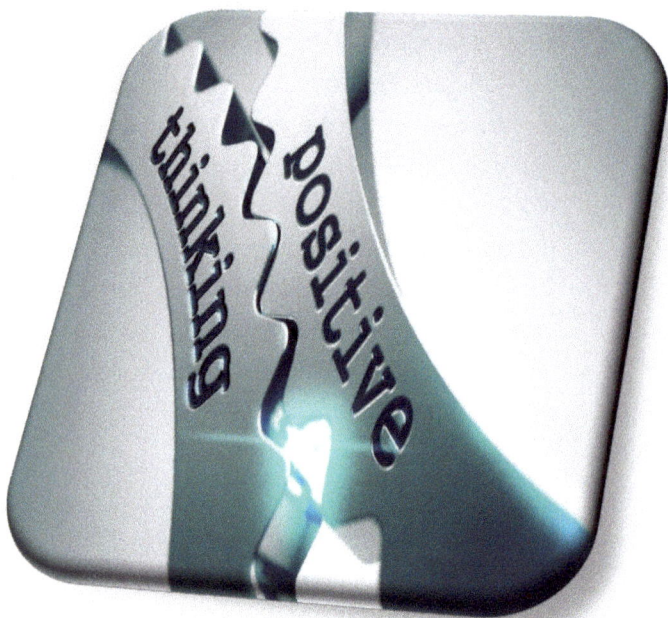

CHAPTER SIX

Managing Your Emotion

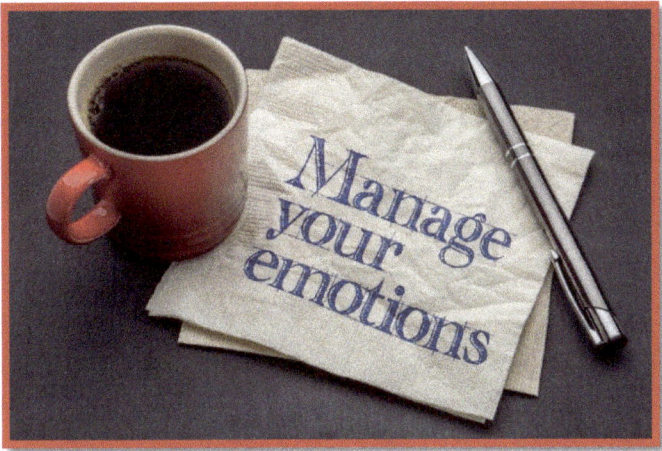

Managing your emotions can positively contribute to living a balanced life. The way you view life's circumstances impact your reactions and consequently your emotions. Keeping a positive outlook will allow you to manage your emotions with greater ease.

Here are five quick tips to develop better control over your emotions:

1. **Learn to respond instead of react.**

Take a moment to pause and consider what just happened, instead of just instantly reacting to new information or a new situation. By taking a few seconds to pause and consider, you can calm yourself briefly, and you will be more likely to produce a better response. So, instead of acting off the cuff, remain calm and respond in a more dignified manner. Thereby, presenting yourself respectfully in the situation and keeping your blood pressure under control!

2. **Focus on what you can control.**

Once you have been presented with a stressful or emotional situation, try to identify what you can and can't control. If something is done, you can't change it. You can only determine what to do **afterward**.

You *can* control your response, and to a certain degree, you can likely control what happens next. By focusing on what you can control, you are empowering yourself. By dwelling on things you can't control, you disempower yourself and make yourself more frustrated and more stressed. Oh, and there goes your blood pressure!

3. **Figure out what's important at that moment.**

When you are presented with a challenging situation in life, it's important to prioritize what things you have to act on right then. If, for example, you arrive at an important meeting, get out of your car, then realize you just locked your keys in the car, what's important at that moment? The meeting is important right then, not your keys. You can deal with the locked car at any time later in the day.

So many people freak out about little urgent matters and lose sight of what's really important for them to focus on first. Again, by taking a few moments to pause and consider, you can refocus your mind on what's most important right then and prioritize your plan of action.

4. Know that you can handle anything.

It's been said that if people made a circle, put their problems in the middle and had to choose a problem to take back out, most people would choose their own problem to retrieve. Whatever challenges you are facing that may cause stress or negative emotions, you can handle them.

5. Change the meaning you give to "negative" events.

The more you practice the points above (especially pausing to respond and realizing that you can handle any challenge), the more you will start to view challenging events as more neutral than negative. You'll even start finding the good in difficult situations, in terms of what lessons you can learn, skills you can develop, and new motivation you can gain.

This skill of turning negative into positive develops like a muscle and becomes almost instinctive over time. Start by saying "No problem" a whole lot more. Pretty soon, you'll condition your mind to believe it.

CONCLUSION

As expressed in each chapter, life is filled with many responsibilities. And, the higher the calling, the more responsibilities one will carry. Beginning each task or new responsibility with the proper mindset is the key to being successful, as well as being mentally and physically healthy.

Recall the parable of the lost son that I shared in the introductory chapter. Three mindsets were presented, but only one of them was healthy- the father's perspective. Although his dear son had departed home without a look back, the father still loved him and held onto the hope that his son would one day return. Like the father, we should always remain positive and keep a healthy outlook, in all that we engage in and/or are challenged with, even when circumstances look bleak or are seemingly unbearable. Having a negative viewpoint will only taint the entire situation.

Proverbs 17:22 says, *"A merry heart doeth good like a medicine: but a broken spirit drieth the bones."*

Keep a healthy spirit and remember James 1:2-8 says, *"My brethren, count it all joy when ye fall into divers temptations; knowing this, that the trying of your faith worketh patience. But let patience have her perfect work, that ye may be perfect and entire, wanting nothing. If any of you lack wisdom, let him ask of God, that giveth to all men liberally, and upbraideth not; and it shall be given him. But let him ask in faith, nothing wavering. For he that wavereth is like a wave of the sea driven with the wind and tossed. For let not that man think that he shall receive any thing of the Lord. A double minded man is unstable in all his ways."*

*Be blessed in all you do,
as you strive to live a balanced, healthy, fulfilled life!*

REFERENCES

Empowering Parents. (2016). *Blended Family? The 5 Secrets of Effective Stepparenting* August 30, 2016. www.empoweringparents.com

"Fool." dictionary.net. July 2006.

"How to Avoid the Naysayers: Eliminating Negative People in Our Lives" September 27, 2006. sumonova.com. August 22, 2016

Perera, Karl. (2003) "Procrastination and Self Esteem!" July 2010.

Gift of Salvation

for Non-Believers

"For all have sinned, and come short of the glory of God."
(Romans 3:23)

This section was written especially for non-believers, those who have not accepted the gift of salvation. The gift of salvation saves souls from eternal damnation and is a free gift offered by God himself.

John 3:16-18 says, *"For God so loved the world, that he gave his only begotten Son, that whosoever believeth in him should not perish, but have everlasting life. For God sent not his Son into the world to condemn the world; but that the world through him might be saved. He that believeth on him is not condemned: but he that believeth not is condemned already, because he hath not believed in the name of the only begotten Son of God."*

This section of scripture tells us God's purpose for giving His son Jesus to the world. The world was in a bad condition. The world was overwrought with sin; the people were living for fleshly desires rather than for God's desires.

As a result of the world's conditions, God decided He would offer the perfect sacrifice that would save the world from being a place where people were lost and had no hope. He decided that His own son could stand in proxy for the sin-filled world, taking all sin upon Himself.

So Jesus came, born of a virgin, to save this dying world. He walked on this earth for 33 ½ years, doing the work of His Heavenly Father. At the appointed time, He died by way of crucifixion upon a cross at Calvary, on Golgatha's hill. He shed his blood and died for you and for me. Because His blood was pure, it paid the penalty for all unrighteousness and gave those who believe in Him direct access to His father's throne.

Scripture tells us in Matthew 27:51 that the veil of the temple was ripped in two from top to bottom, at the moment that Jesus' spirit left His body. As a result of the veil's removal, we are no longer required to have a high priest make intercession for us. We, as the children of the Most High God, are able to approach the throne God for ourselves, and Jesus sits on the right hand of the Father making intercession for us.

But what is even more miraculous than God offering His own son as the perfect sacrifice was the fact that when Jesus was placed in grave clothes and placed in a tomb, He only remained there until the third day. God would not have it that His son would remain in the heart of the earth forever. In order for people to believe in the awesome power of God and His dear son Jesus, a miracle had to be performed. So, on the third day, after Jesus died on the cross, He was resurrected, demonstrating the omnipotence of God. This very act was the act that would cause people to believe in a god that reigns supreme and holds the power of the universe in His very hands, a god that could save them from themselves.

Today, if you are an unbeliever, you can change your destiny. You can change where you will spend your eternity. Our Heavenly Father gives us the freedom of choice about how we want to live our life here on earth and how we want to spend eternity. In Deuteronomy 30:19, God boldly declares, "*I call heaven and earth to record this day against you, that I have set before you life and death, blessing and cursing: therefore choose life, that both thou and thy seed may live.*"

So, dear friend what choice will you make today? Will you spend your eternity with the Creator or will you suffer Hell's eternal flames? Again, the choice is yours. Just as the men aboard the ship who were with Jonah became believers, you too can make a choice to accept the only one and true living God as your god.

If after reading the above passages, you have decided that you want to spend your eternity in Heaven with God, the creator, and His son Jesus, and the Holy Spirit, read through what has affectionately come to be known as the Roman's Road. This is the road to salvation. As you read through the scriptures that comprise the Roman's Road, you will also read the explanation for each scripture so you will have clarity about what you are reading and confessing.

The Roman's Road to Salvation

The road to salvation begins with Romans 3:23 which declares, "*For all have sinned, and come short of the glory of God.*" This scripture explains that everyone has come short of God's glory and needs redemption. Then Romans 6:23a states, "*For the wages of sin is death.*" Here, we learn that the consequence of living a life of sin is death. Everyone will experience physical death as a result of the sin committed in the garden of Eden, but those who commit themselves to a life of sin will suffer eternal damnation in the lake of fire (Rev. 19).

Continue with the rest of verse 6:23 that says, "*but the gift of God is eternal life through Jesus Christ our Lord.*" There is an alternative to suffering eternal damnation. We can accept the gift of salvation by accepting Jesus as our personal lord and savior. Then, Romans 5:8 says, "*But God commendeth his love toward us, in that, while we were yet sinners, Christ died for us.*" We are able to receive the gift of salvation because Christ came to earth and shed His blood for us on the cross.

Continue to Romans 10: 9-10 which says, "*That if thou shalt confess with thy mouth the Lord Jesus, and shalt believe in thine heart that God hath raised him from the dead, thou shalt be saved. For with the heart man believeth unto righteousness; and with the mouth confession is made unto salvation.*" If we confess with our mouths that Jesus is the son of God, that he came and died for our sins, and that God raised Him from the dead, we will receive salvation.

Finish with Romans 10:13, which states, "*For whosoever shall call upon the name of the Lord shall be saved.*" Call upon the name of God by saying these words, "**Lord Jesus, come into my heart and save me Lord. I believe that you are the Son of God who came and died on the cross for my sins. I believe that you rose from the grave. I also believe that you now sit in heaven on the right side of the Father, making intersession for me. I accept you as my Lord and my Savior.**"

Now that you have confessed with your mouth that Jesus is the son of God and that He died for our sins and rose from the grave, **YOU ARE NOW SAVED!!!!** You will spend your eternity in heaven.

The next step is very important- you must find a Bible-based church that teaches the word of God and confesses the Lord Jesus Christ to be the son of God. Don't delay. Do this immediately. Do not leave yourself open to the enemy. Get connected with the saints of the Most High God and keep yourself covered with the unspotted blood of the lamb.

Here is my prayer for you.
Father God,

I thank you for the opportunity to minister your word to the unsaved, the unchurched, and the uncommitted. Father God, I pray now for the souls who have just received the gift of salvation. Lord Father, they have opened their hearts to you, and I know that you have received them into your kingdom and written their names in the Book of Life. Father God, I pray that you will touch their lives and show yourself mightily before them. Let their eyes be opened by the scales falling off, allowing them to see clearly.

Father God, I even pray for the backslider, those who have turned away from you after receiving the gift of salvation. You said in your word that you desire that none would perish. So Lord, I send your word to them right now praying that they would confess the iniquity in their heart, repent, and turn from their evil ways, so that they may receive a life of abundance. You said in your word in Matthew Chapter 14, that every knee shall bow before you and every tongue will confess that Jesus is Lord.

Father God, I pray now that we all come under subjection to your word and that we will humbly submit our lives to you. I ask all these things in the name of my Lord and Savior Jesus Christ.
Amen, Amen, Amen!!!!

I will continue to pray for your success in your walk with God. Remember, this spiritual walk that you are about to embark on will not be an easy walk, but remember, the race is not given to the swift but to those who endure to the end.

Be blessed with heaven's best. I love you!

ABOUT THE AUTHOR

Dr. Cassundra White-Elliott resides in California with her family, where as an English/Education professor she works for various community colleges and universities.

When writing, she writes with the direction of the Holy Spirit, in an effort to share with God's people all that He has for them.

In addition to teaching and writing, Dr. White-Elliott also serves as an evangelistic teacher. She is also the founder of International Women's Commission, a ministry that serves the needs of the entire person, by attending to healing the mind, body, soul, and spirit.

Dr. White-Elliott holds a Ph.D. in Education, a Master's in English Composition, and a Bachelor's in Education.

Dr. White-Elliott is also the founder of CLF Publishing, LLC. For your publishing needs, go online to www.clfpublishing.org.

OTHER BOOKS BY THE AUTHOR

(All books can be purchased at www.creativemindsbookstore.com)

From Despair, through Determination, to Victory!

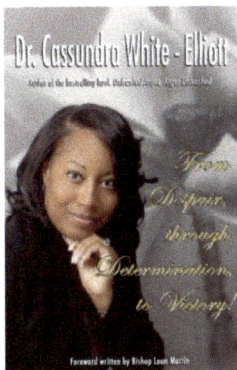

A lot can happen during a span of 40 years. The life of Dr. Cassundra White-Elliott has been anything but uneventful. From a fun-loving childhood sprinkled with incidents of abuse to a tumultuous young adulthood to a stable, secure adult life, she has experienced a full life, with much more to come. Her story is inspiring and motivating.

If anyone lacks hope, reading Dr. White-Elliott's autobiography will propel him/her into an attitude of "Maybe I can." This attitude, if nurtured and developed, will grow into an attitude of "Yes, I can." Throughout her life, Cassundra has always held in her heart the belief that she could achieve anything that she had a made-up mind to embark upon. She was determined to achieve her heart's desires, doing what God has called her to do. She takes no credit for herself. All the glory goes to God, for He is her driving force. In Him, she lives, moves, and has her being.

Through the Storm

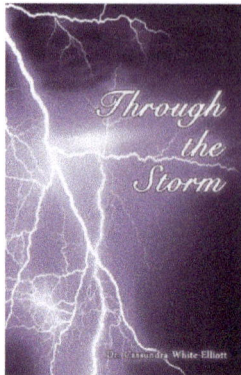

Through the Storm was duly inspired by the avaricious cloud of depression that decided to hover overhead of my daily existence in the latter part of 2007. Although I found it extremely difficult, I was once again compelled to not be defeated by just another snare that the enemy, the trickster, set for me. Once again, or more appropriately I should say *continuously*, he has exerted pernicious efforts to snatch the very life out of me by causing me to wallow in despair and to believe that I had been overcome by failure when in actuality and all reality, I was just experiencing a temporary setback. During those cloudy days, I had to remind myself daily that even though I was a target of the enemy, I am and will always be a child of the Most High god, Jehovah, who is my rock, my stability.

Unleashed Anger, Anger Unleashed

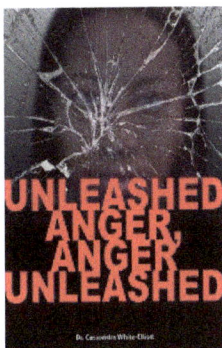

Introduction

What Is This Book All About?

As I prepared to embark upon the adventure of writing this book, I had to prepare myself to also be transparent. I have found that being transparent is required in order for healing to transpire, healing for all those that peruse the pages of this book and myself. And I may as well tell you that today, at the onset of this project, I have not been totally delivered from my condition of being an anger-filled person. However, I am definitely a work in progress. I have made strides with the assistance of my Lord and Savior, Jesus Christ, who is the head of my life. Without his love, guidance, and teachings, I would not be the woman of God I am today. I shudder to think where I could be instead and will therefore not entertain the thought.

Public Speaking in the Spiritual Arena

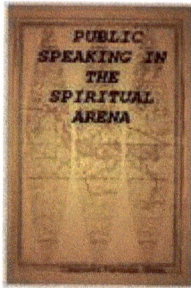

Chapter Two
How Communication Works

Purpose: This chapter will explain the six primary components of communication, identifying their purpose and how they work together.

<u>The Source</u>

In oral communication, the source of information is the speaker. In a church setting, the foundation of the message is God's word, but it is a speaker's interpretation of God's word that is delivered to the audience. As speakers vary, the information may vary but should have a similar essence because the foundational text is the same.

<u>The Message</u>

The message is the collective set of ideas that the speaker (the source) wants to deliver and/or illustrate to the audience. The message can be informative where the speaker informs the audience about a specific set of information. Or, the message may be persuasive in nature if the speaker wants to persuade the audience about conducting themselves in a specific manner, accepting God's commandments, or any number of things.

Where is Your Joppa?

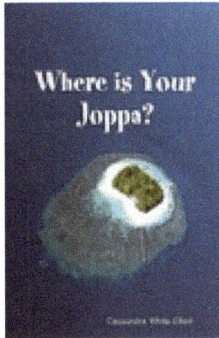

Introduction

Where is Your Joppa? was written for the express purpose of illustrating God's call for obedience in the lives of believers with respect to the individual call that He has on each of our lives. As you read throughout the various chapters, notice that the emphasis is placed on our persistent disobedience in answering God's call in a specific area of our lives. We have become a people who are similar to the Israelites when they found themselves in the middle of the wilderness, following their exodus from Egypt. Before God, they murmured and complained about their current life conditions and failed to be obedient to God's statutes delivered through His servant Moses. Their persistent disobedience caused them to lose the opportunity to see and enter the Promised Land. I ask you, "What has your disobedience cost you?" "Was your disobedience worth what it cost you?" "Do you think about the souls you could have ushered into the kingdom of God?" These are some of the questions that I pray will be answered through your reading of the book.

Mayhem in the Hamptons

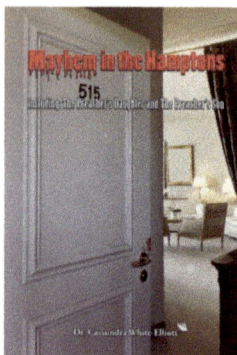

Romero and Yolanda optimistically plan for the day that is going to change their lives from being single persons to a couple who is united in holy matrimony. They, along with their parents, close friends and family, fly over to the infamous Hamptons, where only the rich and famous vacation, to have their dream wedding at the five-star Hampton Suites located on a peninsula in the Hamptons. Little do they know that their perfect day will turn out to be less than perfect when their wedding planner Mariesha Coleman suddenly goes missing!

A time when the newlyweds' lives should be filled with joy and the creation of wonderful memories, they are stricken with grief as they desperately try to find clues to help solve Mariesha's disappearance.

Mayhem in the Hamptons is a tale that shares how the horrors of a woman's past can come back to haunt her in more than one way and the impact it can have on anyone who gets in the way.

Preacher's Daughter

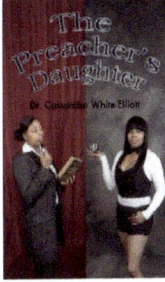

Tinisha, the daughter of a preacher, is a twenty-six year old God-fearing young woman endeavoring to complete law school so that she can make her mark in the courtroom. Working in one of the late-night clubs in Hollywood to earn money to pay her own way through school, Tinisha soon learns that life doesn't always go as planned. Finding her strength in her faith, Tinisha constantly finds herself praying as she watches God move miraculously in her life.

Preacher's Son

Romero Turner is a private investigator with a promising future. As he continues to build his career, he is excited about the cases he undertakes. However, his father Pastor Theodore Turner has other plans for his son's life. In the midst of trying to save his client's husband from Sylvester Domingo, a ruthless crime lord, Romero must try to salvage his relationship with his father. He must decide if ministry or life as a detective is in his future.

Lord, Teach Me to be a Blessing!

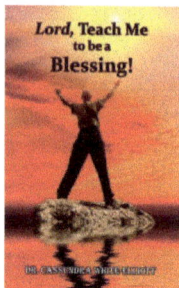

Lord, Teach Me to be a Blessing! will change a person's mentality from being centered around "me, myself, and I" to focusing on "others."

The world system teaches us that it is acceptable to place ourselves above others in an attempt to get ahead and even to survive. Herbert Spencer coined the phrase '*survival of the fittest*' after reading Charles Darwin's theory of evolution. This concept of surpassing and outdoing others is the world's philosophy.

However, the word of God does not subscribe to or promote this self-centered ideology, and therefore, neither should believers. We must hold fast to the truths outlined in Holy Scripture: "*Love thy neighbor as you love thyself*" (James 2:8) and "*It is more blessed to give than to receive*" (Acts 20:35).

While holding God's truths to be self-evident, we must demonstrate them to others, thereby showing them the way of the Lord of how to be a blessing to someone *rather* than looking to receive a blessing.

This is the very purpose of this book: to change the mentality of the world from being *self*-centered to *other* centered.

After the Dust Settles

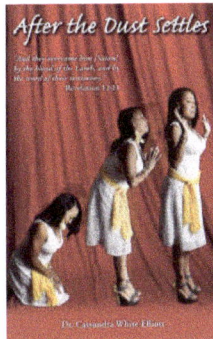

Throughout the journey of life, we all experience ups and downs and joys and pains. Most of us successfully find solutions to the situations/problems we encounter, but we often avoid dealing with the attached emotions. If we continue to ignore the emotions of pain, hurt, disappointment, anger, etc., we set ourselves up for destruction. Our families, our cultures, and our society tell us to be strong, to keep our chin up, and to grin and bear it. However, these methods of avoidance can lead us to strokes due to the undue amount of pressure we place on ourselves and/or mental illness from being unable to cope with the emotional baggage we have accumulated.

In *After the Dust Settles,* Dr. C. White-Elliott shares several situations that we all may encounter at one time or another in our lifetime and how to successfully navigate through them, so we can find ourselves emotionally healthy after the dust has settled and the situation has been rectified.

Begin reading today and experience a better tomorrow!

A Diamond in the Rough

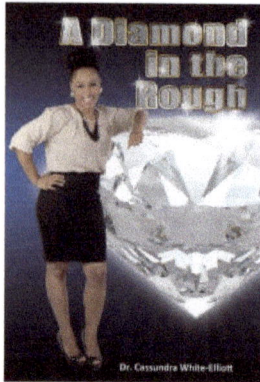

A Diamond in the Rough Architecture Firm was built and is owned and operated by lead architect Kyra Fraser. For the last five years, Kyra has been extremely successful in business, but her love life leaves much to be desired.

Kyra has set high standards for herself and does not wish to take a man in any condition and attempt to make him over. She is looking for someone who is drama free, well educated, very cultured, fun-loving, good looking, self-motivated, and the list goes on.

Will Kyra find the man of her dreams, or will her dream just continue to be a dream?

As you delve into this page-turning novel, Kyra's reality will unfold as you are drawn into her world of design, love and office drama- which includes her best friend's husband who is looking for love in all the wrong places.

365 Days of Encouragement

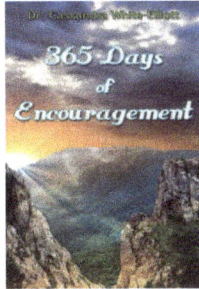

Just as our brain requires oxygen obtained from the air we breathe to sustain our mortal bodies, our spirit requires revitalization and encouragement in order to be strengthened each and every day of our lives. The revitalization and encouragement needed for the spirit of man comes directly from the word of God and assists us in walking according to the way of our heavenly Father. 365 Days of Encouragement provides a scripture a day for each day of the year. Along with the daily scripture is a brief note of commentary also for the benefit of edifying the saints of God.

It is my prayer that the people of God would live a fulfilled life through Christ Jesus. Knowing His word and understanding we can walk in the fulfillment thereof is empowering. We are instructed in II Timothy 2:15, "Study to shew thyself approved unto God, a workman that needeth not to be ashamed, rightly dividing the word of truth" (KJV). Take an opportunity to delve further into the word of God, to know His statutes and to allow your own personal life to be edified, so you can be equipped to bring glory to God and lived a fulfilled life.

A Mother's Heart

A Mother's Heart shares the unconditional love of mothers through a compilation of testimonies. Each testimony serves as a tribute to a special mother. The children of the represented mothers have lovingly written about their childhood, young adult life and/or older adult experiences they shared with their mother. As you read the writers' reflections, you will feel the expressions of love exude from the pages.

The purpose of this book is two-fold. First, it honors those mothers who stood by their children through the trials of life and showered them with unconditional love. Second, the book is a source of encouragement for mothers who may feel inadequate and question whether or not they are actually suited for motherhood. Our advice to mothers is, "Be encouraged; the journey of motherhood may seem daunting at times and you may shed some tears, but your children will never forget the love you have shown them and instilled in them to share with others."

Mothers may not be perfect, but they are definitely unmatched by any other category of person on God's green earth!

Broken Chains

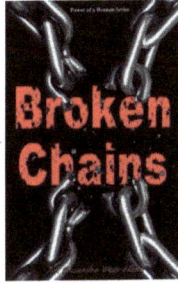

Broken Chains is an in-depth survey of five life-changing tragedies that can and will serve as chains to bind us if we are not watchful and mindful of their potential effects. In our lifetimes, we may all experience death of loved ones, sexual abuse, broken relationships, promiscuity, and sickness and disease. These everyday life occurrences can have detrimental effects on the remaining years of our lives and change our existence, unless we deal with them in a healthy manner.

Broken Chains not only brings to light the detrimental effects of five life-changing tragedies, but it also shares how anyone who experiences them can be healed and delivered from their effects.

If you have experienced death of a loved one, sexual abuse, a broken relationship, the effects of promiscuity, and/or sickness and disease and have not been able to rid yourself of the emotions attached to them or specific resulting behaviors, Broken Chains is for you.

God designed each of us for a purpose, and He has an intended end for us to achieve. In order for us to effectively achieve our God-given purpose, we must be free of chains that bind us. It is not God's desire that we become immobilized by life's events. His desire is for us to be healed, delivered and set free. Be healed today, in the name of the Lord Jesus Christ!

I Have Fallen

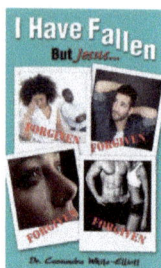

Do you know anyone who has committed his/her life to Christ but has done something unseemly that you would never expect a Christian to do? How did you feel about that person or what the person did? Did you pass judgment? What if that person were you? How would you feel if you made a misstep and no one forgave you and instead began to treat you differently? How do you feel when you are judged for past mistakes or lifestyles that are no longer part of your life?

This book shares four true stories of Christians who have made missteps during their walk with God. The purpose is not to air their dirty laundry, but to demonstrate our humanness and our vulnerability. None of us are exempt from making errors and falling into sin. It can happen to any of us.

The solution for these dilemmas is for the person who fell into sin to make a life-changing move and turn away from the sin, repent and ask God for forgiveness. His arms are waiting!

The next solution is for those who witness the sin or know of it. Pray and be of comfort to the one who has fallen. Lead him/her back to the path of righteousness. Love thy neighbor and treat him/her as you want to be treated!

The Bottom Line

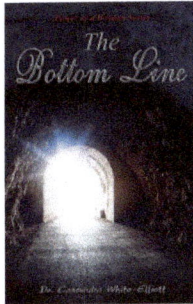

The Bottom Line is a detailed review of the Book of Job. Much can be said about Job's experiences with the loss of his children and wealth and the subsequent return of it all in mass proportions. However, the telling of Job's story in the Holy writ was not intended to focus on the return of his wealth. Instead, the focal point should be on the bottom line of the entire situation.

When you experience trials or tragedies in your life, do you tend to focus on the trial itself, the result, or the bottom line?

"What is the bottom line?" you may ask. The bottom line is the message God is sending regarding the situation.

When Job experienced his tragedies, there was a bottom line. Likewise, when you experience your trials and tragedies, there is a bottom line as well. It is up to you to discover it.

This book will reveal the bottom line in the Book of Job. It is readily apparent, but many often overlook it.

Now, it is up to you to uncover the bottom line of your experiences, for God will not bring a trial to you without a good reason.

Power of a Woman

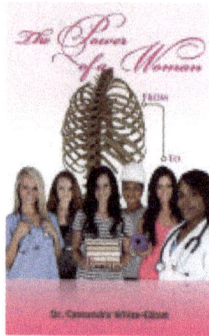

The ongoing conversation about the value of a woman is presented from a different perspective in The Power of a Woman. Dr. Cassundra White-Elliott presents a biblical perspective of women and compares it to the worldview of both yesterday and today. This comparison seeks to illustrate God's intended purpose for His uniquely designed creation: woman. Dr. Elliott shares God's truth about pre-imposed limitations set by man versus the limitations God Himself set for woman in addition to the wealth of liberality He gave her.

Women's creativity and abilities are not meant to be stifled. They are meant to be utilized to bring glory to God, to help sustain and nurture their families, and to move the world forward. Knowing God's truth will show women how to celebrate and appreciate who they are as well as one another!

Women, let's take the blinders off, lift our heads up, and march forward, side by side with men, and bring glory and honor to God! Take your rightful place with a gentle smile and grace and be who God called you to be!

Set Free

If you possess habits and display characteristics that are unbecoming, debilitating, and hinder the desired progress in your life or that affect your relationships with others, Set Free will provide the steps you need to be healed and delivered, through the Word of God.

Deliverance is available to you! Claim your healing today and walk in victory!

Do You Know God?

Have you or someone you know ever felt alone, confused, or unsure about your walk with God or are you unsure of what being a Christian is all about? *Do You Know God?* is an excellent text for providing answers to many of your questions. This book introduces adolescents and young adults to God in addition to answer many of their questions about being a Christian. This book shares the testimonies of the trials and tribulations that other teens have experienced and how God prevailed in their lives. All the information that is shared on the pages of the book is based upon the Word of God and the scriptures are taken from the King James Version of the Bible. If you are interested in knowing more about God's Word or how to begin your Christian experience, this book is for you.